What Do You Call a Group of Turkeys?

And Other Bird Groups

EMMA NATHAN

BLACKBIRCH PRESS, INC.

WOODBRIDGE, CONNECTICUT

Published by Blackbirch Press, Inc.
260 Amity Road
Woodbridge, CT 06525
web site: http://www.blackbirch.com
e-mail: staff@blackbirch.com

© 2000 Blackbirch Press, Inc.
First Edition

Printed in Singapore

10 9 8 7 6 5 4 3 2 1

Photo Credits
Cover, pages 3, 4, 7, 13, 19, 21: ©Photodisc; pages 5, 6, 9, 10, 11, 14, 15, 20: ©Corel Corporation; page 8: ©Robert M. Ballou/Animals Animals; pages 12, 18: ©Art Wolfe/Art Wolfe, Inc./Photo Researchers, Inc.; pages 16, 22: ©Digital Stock Corporation; page 17: ©Corbis Corporation.

Library of Congress Cataloging-in-Publication Data
Nathan, Emma.
          What do you call a group of turkeys? : and other bird groups / by Emma Nathan.
          p. cm.— (What do you call a —)
Includes index.
Summary: Explains the terms used for groups of birds, including parrots, cranes, and penguins and provides information on the group behavior of these creatures.
          ISBN 1-56711-357-5 (hardcover : alk. paper)
          1. Birds—Miscellanea—Juvenile literature. 2. English language—Collective nouns—Juvenile literature. [1. Birds—Miscellanea.
2. English language—Collective nouns. 3. Questions and answers.] I. Title
QL676.2 .N29   2000   00-008223
598—dc21   CIP

Contents

What do you call a group of turkeys?

What Do You Know?

Happy Ever Rafter

Turkeys like to gather in small groups in the forest. During mating season, the males attract females to the area with their loud gobbling. Some of this gobbling can be heard up to a mile away! Although they roost in trees at night, turkeys build their nests on the ground.

A group of turkeys is called a rafter.

What do you call   a group of penguins**?**

She Lays, He Stays

Penguins like to gather in very large groups. Each year, thousands of penguins return to the same rookery, which is where they lay their eggs. Some rookeries can be home to more than 1 million birds! At an emperor penguin rookery, the female lays an egg and gives it to her mate. The male then keeps the egg warm under a flap of skin until it hatches. Meanwhile, the female goes back to the sea, but the male stays with the egg. He goes without a single bite of food until the chick has hatched!

What do you call a group of owls?

7

An Owl on the Prowl

Owls usually live alone, except during mating season. At that time, a male and a female remain together while they incubate their eggs and raise their young (called owlets). Most owls are nocturnal, which means they are active at night. While they hunt, they use their large eyes and excellent night vision to see the movements of rodents and other small prey.

What do you call a group of chickens?

⬧⬧WHAT DO YOU KNOW?⬧⬧

Peep Peep, Hooray

Chickens are probably the most common birds on Earth. Like other birds, chickens will naturally flock together for safety. When they do, each chicken gains protection—being part of a large group makes it harder to be seen by an enemy. A peep is specifically a collection or group of young chicks.

What do you call a group of storks?

❖❖ WHAT DO YOU KNOW? ❖❖

Stork Station

Storks are mostly found in pairs. Like many birds, they will mate for life, and males and females will share in the raising of young. Mating pairs of storks return to the same nest every year. Nests are most often built in high trees or steep cliffs. Storks are mute, which means they cannot make sounds with their throats. They share this trait with their cousins, the vultures.

What do you call a group of parrots?

··WHAT DO YOU KNOW?··

A Tropical Parrot-dise

Parrots are noisy, social birds that live in forested areas—mostly in tropical climates. More than half of the 315 species of parrots are found in Central and South America. These birds pair off for life, and many pairs will often gather together to form large groups. At night, parrots will form "roosting groups." Staying together offers protection to each of the members while they sleep.

A group of parrots is called a company

What do you call a group of swans **?**

It Takes Swan to Know One

Swans like to be organized into groups while they travel. Like ducks and geese, swans fly in a neat, V-shaped formation. Most males and females will mate for life and will share the duties of building a nest and raising their young. The males and females of most bird species look very different. With swans, however, it is nearly impossible to tell a male and female apart.

What do you call a group of cranes**?**

Crane and Simple

Cranes gather together in groups mostly during mating season. Marshy areas and wetlands are the habitats that suit cranes best. There, they grab fish with their long beaks and eat a variety of insects. Cranes are some of the tallest birds on Earth. The whooping crane is the tallest bird in North America—it is also an endangered species.

What do you call a group of ducks?

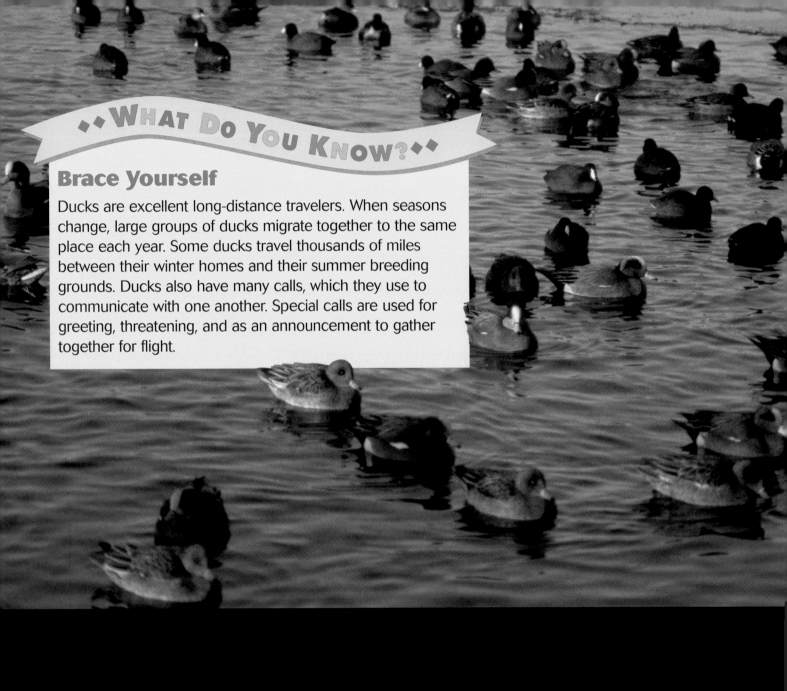

•• WHAT DO YOU KNOW? ••

Brace Yourself

Ducks are excellent long-distance travelers. When seasons change, large groups of ducks migrate together to the same place each year. Some ducks travel thousands of miles between their winter homes and their summer breeding grounds. Ducks also have many calls, which they use to communicate with one another. Special calls are used for greeting, threatening, and as an announcement to gather together for flight.

What do you call a group of geese?

Increase the Geese

Geese like to travel in a well-organized, V-shaped formation. They also prefer to remain in groups while they feed. As the group feeds, one goose will stand guard and will alert the others if danger approaches. Geese are good swimmers and very strong fliers. Some geese have been known to fly as high as 29,000 feet (8,839 meters)!

A group of geese is called a flock, a gaggle, or a skein.

Some Other Bird Groups

Flock	**Muster**	**Bevy**	**Siege**
chickens	*storks*	*swans*	*cranes*
geese	peacocks	quail	herons
wrens			
swifts			

Glossary

Breeding ground—a place where male and female animals produce their young.

Endangered species—a plant or animal that is in danger of becoming extinct.

Gobbling—the sound a turkey makes.

Incubate—to keep eggs warm before they hatch.

Mating season—the time when male and female animals raise their young.

Migrate—when birds fly away at a certain time of the year to live somewhere else.

Nocturnal—an animal that is active at night.

Prey—an animal that is hunted by another for food.

Rookery—a place where birds lay their eggs.

Roost—a place where birds rest for the night.

Trait—a feature that makes one thing different from another.

Wetlands—land, which has very moist soil.

For More Information

Books

Latimer, Jonathan P., Karen Stray Nolting, and Roger Tory Peterson. *Birds of Prey* (Peterson Field Guides for Young Naturalists). Boston, MA: Houghton Mifflin Co., 1999.

Miller, Sarah Swan. *Waterfowl: From Swans to Screamers* (Animals in Order). Danbury, CT: Franklin Watts, Inc., 1999.

Rauzon, Mark J. *Parrots* (First Book). Danbury, CT: Franklin Watts, Inc., 1996.

Stefoff, Rebecca. *Owl* (Living Things). Tarrytown, NY: Benchmark Books, 1997.

Weidensaul, Scott, Annette Tison, and Talus Taylor. *Birds* (National Audubon Society First Field Guides). New York, NY: Scholastic Trade, 1998.

Video

Smithsonian Video Library Series—Penguin World (Smithsonian), 1992.

Web Sites

Bird of the Week
Find out information on a different bird each week—
www.birds.cornell.edu/bow

Ducks at a Distance
Learn about the various species of ducks and geese—
www.npwrc.usgs.gov/resource/tools/duckdist/duckdist.htm

Index